KU-167-597

Bits and Pieces

Start collecting bits and pieces to make the wonderful pictures in this book. You'll need paper and card, wool and felt, sequins and beads, foil, glitter and paints, sponge and fancy sweet wrappers.

You can either make the pictures just the same as the ones in the book, or you can use the ideas to design your own. There are all sorts of exciting and unusual painting techniques for you to try out as well.

Acknowledgements

Designed by **Jane Warring**
Illustrations by **Lindy Norton**
Pictures made by **Karen Radford**
Photographs by **Peter Millard**
Created by **Thumbprint Books**

First published in 1994 by
Hamlyn Children's Books
an imprint of Reed Children's Books,
Michelin House, 81 Fulham Road, London SW3 6RB
and Auckland, Melbourne, Sydney and Toronto

Copyright © 1994 Thumbprint Books

All rights reserved. No part of this publication may be reproduced, stored in a retrieval system, or transmitted, in any form or by any means, electronic, mechanical, photocopying, recording, or otherwise, without prior permission of the copyright holders.

ISBN 0600 58289 2

Printed and bound in Belgium by Proost

Making Pictures
AMAZING ANIMALS

Penny King and Clare Roundhill

Contents

HAMLYN

Crazy Caterpillar

Make this crazy caterpillar out of red and green felt or any other bright fabric.

To make the picture extra smart, give it a fingerprint border (see paint tip).

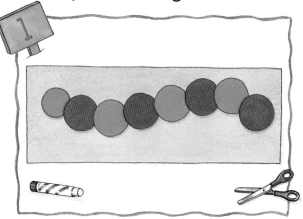

Cut out eight felt circles for the body and head. Overlap and glue them on the yellow card.

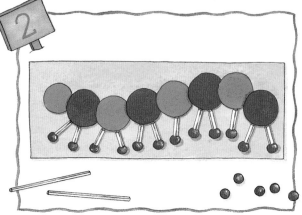

Cut the straws into 12 short legs. Glue them to the body. Stick on shiny red bead boots.

Bits and Pieces

- Red and green felt
- Yellow card
- 3 drinking straws
- Shiny red beads
- Scissors
- Glue
- Strips of coloured paper
- Paint
- Paper stars
- Sequins

PAINT TIP
Dip the tip of your index finger into red paint. Press it on to the yellow card. Dip your middle finger into green paint. Make a print next to the red one. Repeat.

Make the antennae from strips of folded paper and glue them on. Stick beads on the tips.

Decorate the caterpillar's body with paper stars. Stick on a paper mouth and sequin eyes.

7

Spring Sheep

These fluffy sheep would make a good Easter card for your family or friends. If you can find some real sheep's wool, this is even better for making their bodies than cotton wool. Put the sheep in a grassy field full of spring flowers.

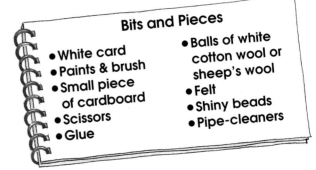

Bits and Pieces
- White card
- Paints & brush
- Small piece of cardboard
- Scissors
- Glue
- Balls of white cotton wool or sheep's wool
- Felt
- Shiny beads
- Pipe-cleaners

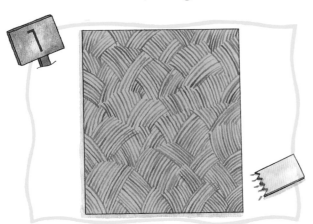

Make a grassy background for your sheep to graze on (see paint tip). Leave it to dry.

For each sheep's body, glue small cotton wool balls close together on the grassy field.

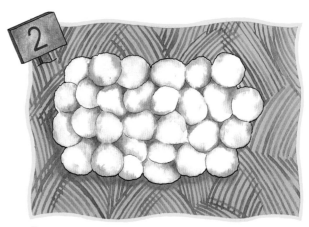

Cut heads and legs from black felt. Glue them in place. Stick on shiny beads for their eyes.

Glue lots of bright felt flowers in between the sheep. Give them pipe-cleaner stalks and leaves.

PAINT TIP
Cut zig-zags along one edge
of the small piece of cardboard to make a comb. Cover
the white card all over with
thick green paint. Use the
comb to make wavy grass
shapes in the wet paint.

9

Contented Cats

Why not make these two soft, furry, wool cats sitting on top of a garden wall?

Add some bright yellow tissue flowers to give your picture extra colour.

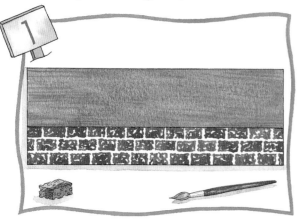

Print bricks along the bottom of the card (see paint tip). Paint a pale blue sky on the top half.

Cut cat shapes out of black or brown card. Glue wool in lines or spirals all over them.

PAINT TIP
Cut a small rectangle out of sponge. Soak it in water and then squeeze it dry. Press it lightly in brown paint. Starting at the bottom left-hand corner of the white card, print rows of bricks, leaving a small space between each one.

10

Bits and Pieces

- Cellulose sponge
- Scissors
- Old saucer
- Paints & brush
- Stiff white, brown and black card
- A pencil
- Scraps of wool
- Glue
- Pink felt
- Beads
- Tissue paper

3

Add pink felt noses, woolly whiskers and bead eyes. Then stick the cats on top of the wall.

4

Glue on flowers made from circles of yellow tissue with black centres and twisted tissue stalks.

A Proud Peacock

Raid the sewing basket for scraps of patterned fabric to make this peacock with a magnificent tail. Use lots of different colours for the feathers. To make him look really proud, outline him with gold glitter standing on a grassy background.

Bits and Pieces

- Stiff white card
- Wax crayons
- Paints & brush
- Blue and green fabric scraps
- Felt
- Scissors & glue
- Red sequins
- Gold paper
- Red and gold pipe-cleaners
- Gold glitter

Make a grassy background on the card for your peacock to stand on (see paint tip).

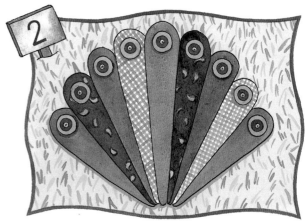

Overlap and glue fabric tail feathers on to the background. Add felt and sequin 'eyes'.

Cut out a blue fabric head and body. Stick it over the feathers. Glue on red pipe-cleaner feet.

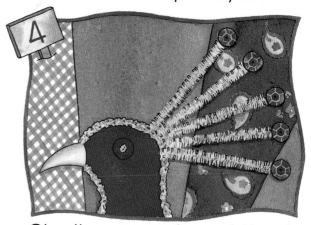

Give the peacock a gold beak, sequin eye and head-feathers made of glittery pipe-cleaners.

PAINT TIP
Use wax crayons to draw
short blades of grass in
yellow and different shades
of green all over the stiff
white card. Brush a coat of
watery green paint on top.
Leave it to dry.

13

A Dangerous Dragon

Transform a cardboard roll, yoghurt pot and egg boxes into a fire-breathing dragon.

Paint him green and then decorate him with button eyes and beads or sweets.

Paint the egg boxes (see paint tip), loo roll and yogurt pot for the dragon's head and body.

Cut tissue strips. Snip one edge to make a fringe. Tape them to the boxes and the yogurt pot.

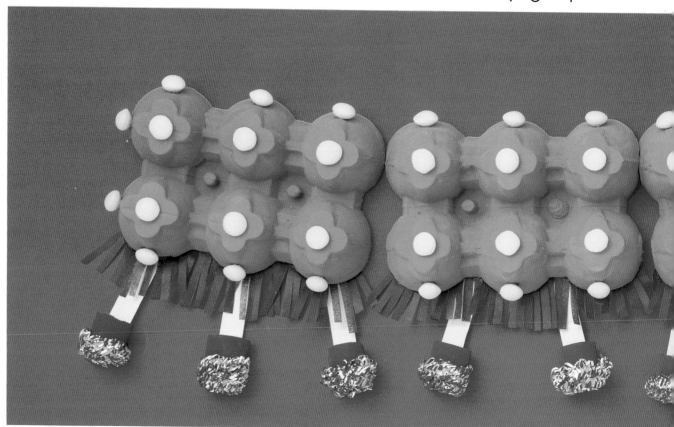

Bits and Pieces

- Bottoms of three egg boxes
- Loo roll tube
- Small yogurt pot
- Paints & brush
- Tissue paper
- Scissors
- Glue & tape
- Pipe-cleaners
- Buttons & beads
- Red card
- Chicken frills

PAINT TIP
To paint egg boxes, use a fat brush and thick paint. Squash the tip of the brush into the holes and wiggle it about. Let the paint dry before you glue on the beady spots.

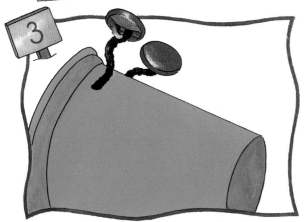

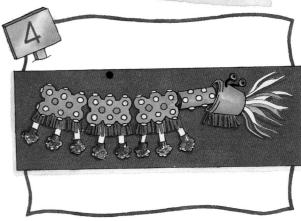

Make eyes from pipe-cleaners and buttons. Pierce holes in the pot and poke them through.

Glue the dragon on to the card. Add paper legs, chicken frill feet, tissue flames and spots.

15

A Zippy Zebra

Use strips of torn newspaper and magazine pages to create this amazing zebra galloping through the African grasslands. Draw round a small plate on to white card or paper to make the full moon and fill the sky with sparkling stars.

Bits and Pieces

- White paper
- Plate
- Pencil
- Scissors
- Paints & brush
- Silver glitter
- PVA glue
- Black card
- Newspaper and old magazines
- Silver foil
- Sticky silver stars

Cut out a big moon from white paper. Paint it (see paint tip). Glue it on to the black card.

Draw a zebra on newspaper. Glue on darker stripes torn from old magazines. Cut it out.

Stick the zebra on to the card. Tear newspaper grass strips and glue them across the picture.

Cut out silver foil stars. Glue them all over the sky along with some ready-made sticky stars.

PAINT TIP
To make grey paint, mix a dab of black into a large splodge of white. Starting at the centre of the moon, paint round in a spiral. Sprinkle glitter on while the paint is still wet, to make it glisten.

17

Darting Dragonflies

Dainty dragonflies, dancing and darting over a pond make a wonderful picture.

Use wax and paint for the water. Stick on dragonflies with see-through wings.

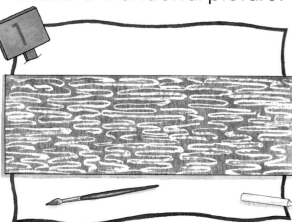

Paint a watery blue and white background for your picture (see paint tip). Leave it to dry.

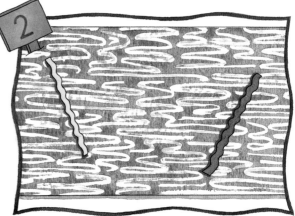

Cut a length of ric-rac for each dragonfly's body. Glue them at angles on to the water.

Bits and Pieces

- White card
- White candle
- Paint & brush
- Coloured ric-rac
- Scissors
- Coloured glitter
- Glue
- Paper doilies
- Sweet wrappers
- Sequins
- Coloured card
- Pipe-cleaners

PAINT TIP
Draw a rippling pond on the card with the end of a candle. Press quite hard. Cover the card with watered down blue paint. You will find that the ripples show through.

Cut out sweet wrapper wings. Glue them in place and highlight with glitter. Add sequin eyes.

Cut out card and pipe-cleaner bullrushes and tall green reeds. Glue them at the water's edge.

19

A Rugged Reindeer

Create a really different Christmas picture of a handsome reindeer made out of lots of tiny crumpled tissue balls. Give it big handprint antlers and a bright red nose. Set it against a background of sparkling snow and ice.

Bits and Pieces
- Brown paint
- Paintbrush
- White paper
- Scissors
- White card
- PVA glue
- Sugar or salt
- Silver glitter
- Pencil
- Brown, red and blue tissue paper

Make antlers with handprints (see paint tip). Leave them to dry before you cut them out.

Cover the card with PVA glue. Sprinkle sugar and glitter on top. Shake off any extra bits.

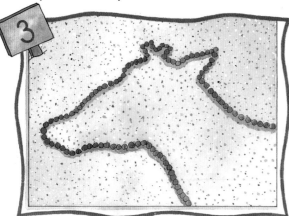

Crumple small pieces of brown tissue into balls. Stick them down to make an outline of the head.

Fill in the head. Use blue for the eye and red for the nose. Glue the antlers on top of the head.

PAINT TIP
Paint your left hand brown. Press it down on some white paper, with your fingers spread out, to make a handprint Then paint your right hand and make another handprint.

21

Funny Frogs

These croaking frogs sitting on lily pads floating in a pond make a funny picture.

Decorate the edge of the pond with green paper reeds and a glowing sun.

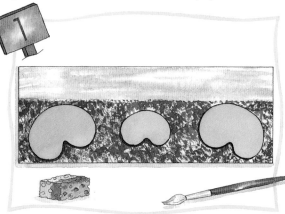

Paint the white card (see paint tip). Glue on three green paper lily pads, two big and one small.

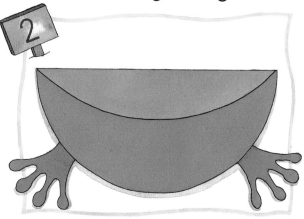

Cut dark green card circles for the frogs. Fold each one in half. Glue on big green paper feet.

PAINT TIP
Thoroughly wet the white card all over with a damp sponge. Quickly brush strokes of light blue paint across the card. Let it dry. Then dip a small sponge in darker blue paint. Dab it over the bottom half of the card to make ripples of water in a pond.

Bits and Pieces

- Long piece of stiff white card
- Paints & brush
- Jar of water
- Cellulose sponge
- Scissors
- Pencil
- Green, yellow and black paper
- Glue
- Pipe-cleaners
- Sticky tape

Make yellow paper eyes with black pupils, like this. Bend and glue them to the frogs' heads.

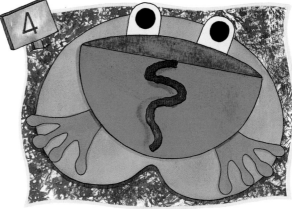

Tape a pipe-cleaner tongue inside each frog's mouth. Stick the frogs on to the lily pads.

23

Perching Parrot

Create a crazy, colourful parrot, like this, with rows and rows of bright tissue feathers. Give him a leafy green background and a real twig to perch on. Instead of using tissue feathers you could paint your parrot bold colours.

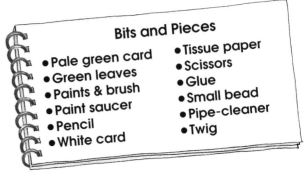

Bits and Pieces
- Pale green card
- Green leaves
- Paints & brush
- Paint saucer
- Pencil
- White card
- Tissue paper
- Scissors
- Glue
- Small bead
- Pipe-cleaner
- Twig

Print a leafy background in different shades of green (see paint tip). Leave it to dry.

Draw a parrot on white card. Paint it and cut it out. Stick on rows of zig-zag tissue feathers.

Cut long tissue tail feathers in different colours. Glue them in place. Stick on a bead eye.

Wrap a pipe-cleaner claw around a twig. Glue the twig and parrot on to the leafy card.

PAINT TIP
To make leaf prints, paint
the bumpy side of a leaf.
Holding the stalk, place
the painted leaf on to
the card. Use your other
hand to press down the
leaf. Lift it off carefully.

Busy Bugs

Make a bright and busy picture of bugs, beetles and crawly caterpillars.

Cut them out of felt and colourful paper. Glue them on to flowers and leaves.

1

Paint a grassy background in different shades of green on the white card (see paint tip).

2

Cut out colourful card leaves, flowers and stalks. Stick them on the grassy background.

Bits and Pieces

- White card
- Paints & brush
- Palette or plate
- Coloured card
- Different coloured felt
- Scissors
- PVA glue
- Pen
- Pipe-cleaners
- Beads
- Shiny paper

PAINT TIP
To make blades of grass, dip the tip of a paintbrush into green paint. Dab it with quick flicks all over the card. Space out the flicks. Fill in the spaces with different greens.

3

4

Draw beetles, bees, caterpillars and other crawling bugs on coloured felt. Cut them out.

Glue them on the plants. Add pipe-cleaner antennae, bead eyes, spots, stripes and wings.

27

Enormous Elephants

To make both elephants the same size, fold a big piece of white paper in half.

Draw an elephant on the top half. Then cut out both layers at the same time.

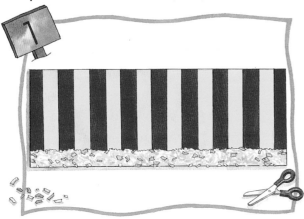

Glue red paper stripes on the yellow card. Spread glue along the bottom. Stick on sawdust.

Make two elephants (see paint tip). Stick them on the card with their feet on the sawdust.

PAINT TIP
Draw an elephant and a separate ear shape on a big piece of white card. Cut them out. Wet a sponge and squeeze it dry. Dip it in grey paint. Dab it gently all over the elephants and their ears. Try the effect on a sheet of spare paper first.

Bits and Pieces

- Yellow card
- Red paper
- PVA glue
- Sawdust
- White card
- Pencil
- Scissors
- Grey paint
- Small sponge
- Black beads
- Bright paper
- Sequins & glitter

3 Glue an ear on each elephant. Stick on a white card tusk and a black bead eye as well.

4 Cut out bright paper blankets. Glue them on the elephants' backs. Add sequins and glitter.